D1088788

CAMERA ON GHANA

The World of a Young Fisherman

CAMERA ON GHANA

The World of a Young Fisherman

BY VICTOR ENGLEBERT

HARCOURT BRACE JOVANOVICH, INC.   NEW YORK

Curriculum-Related Books are relevant to current interests
of young people and to topics in the school curriculum.

First Edition

ISBN 0-15-214069-7

Library of Congress Catalog Card Number: 76-151025

Printed in the United States of America

TO VERONIQUE

CAMERA ON GHANA

The World of a Young Fisherman

Kwabla is a familiar figure on the beach of Atorkor, a small fishing village on the coast of Ghana. He wants to be a fisherman one day, and he spends almost every spare moment on the beach, helping the older men or playing with his friends. On this sunny afternoon, Kwabla is very proudly carrying home a large fish, which he got as payment for his help.

4

Kwabla's father, Togbi Awusa II, is the chief of Atorkor. Unlike most of the men in Atorkor, who are fishermen, he is a farmer. As chief of Atorkor, Togbi Awusa II is the head of the Council of Elders, which governs the village. He also represents the village before the national government.

He is highly respected by the people and spends much of his time discussing village matters with them. Here he hammers home a point as he talks with two men who have come to ask his advice.

5

Kwabla and his family belong to the Ewe tribe, the largest in the southeastern region of Ghana, and they follow many traditions that are centuries old. In Ghana, for example, each child is given several names, and one is always the name of the day on which he was born. Kwabla's name means Tuesday.

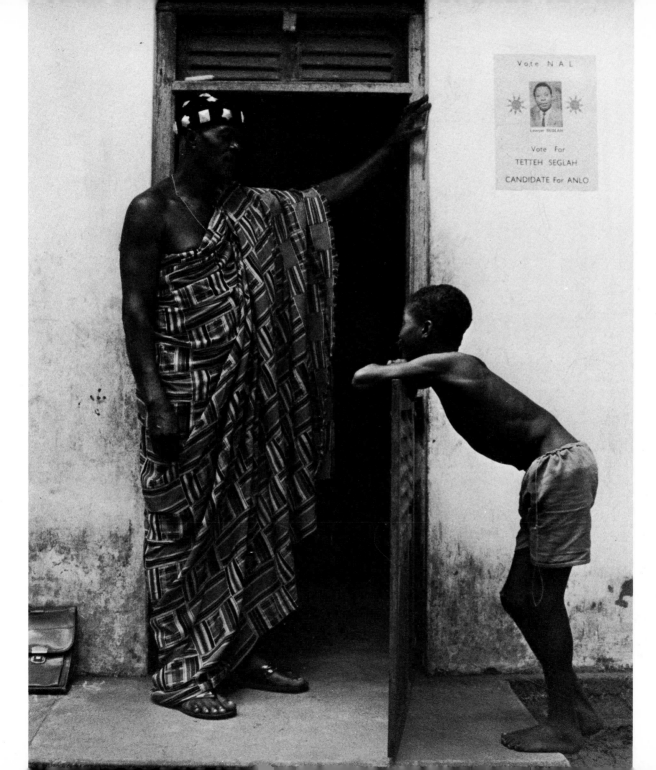

Kwabla's family—he, his parents, his brother, his younger sister, his married sister, and her husband and children—fill three houses, which are built around an open yard and enclosed by a wall. Much of the cooking is done in the yard under the shade of palm trees. Here stand the family's well, two ovens to smoke fish, a fireplace, and a small stone mill to crush peppers and tomatoes.

The day begins early in Atorkor. Kwabla and his sister's son, Kofi, fold the straw mat they share at night. They sweep their room and the front steps of their house. After a quick breakfast of corn porridge, the boys walk a short distance to the beach, where the men have gathered for the day's fishing.

The fishermen have already loaded the net in their boat, and Kwabla and Kofi help them push it into the shallow water.

The men must wait for exactly the right moment to launch the boat. When the water becomes still between waves, the fishermen give a strong push and leap into the boat. Then, matching their strokes to a shouted rhythm, they quickly paddle out beyond the surf.

A boy of fourteen or fifteen then dives from the boat, holding a rope attached to the net, and swims ashore. Later the men will use this rope to pull in one side of the net.

The men in the boat paddle parallel to the shore, dropping the large net as they go. Lead weights at the bottom of the net and floaters at the top hold it extended in the water. When it is completely in place, the men paddle back to shore with a rope attached to the other side of the net.

Like surfers, they ride the waves and pull the boat onto the sand.

The fishermen patiently pull the net back to shore inch by inch. It will take them three or four hours to land their catch.

Kwabla and Kofi would like to stay to watch the fishing net come in, but by 7:30 they must be on their way to school.

At school the classes are taught in English, Ghana's official language, although at home Kwabla and his friends speak Ewe, the language of their tribe.

By mid-morning, more men have come to help pull in the net, which is now heavy with fish. On each side of the net, a man coils the rope to keep it from getting tangled.

Around eleven, women start coming to the beach. Some are fishermen's wives, who will take home their husbands' share of the catch. Others come from Atorkor and neighboring villages to buy fish. They all bring large enamel pans, baskets, and pails for carrying the fish, which they will later sell in nearby markets.

Since Kwabla's father is a farmer, his mother comes to the beach every day to buy fish for the family. Like this woman, she brings with her some bananas, oranges, and a hard corn porridge called kenkey to sell to the hungry fishermen.

The beach is soon crowded with people.

When the sides of the net reach the men's hands, they pull hard but very slowly, so that they will not scare the fish or break the net. A few men wade into the surf to lift and roll the sides of the net.
As the net approaches the shore, the two lines of men move closer together.

Soon the lines cross and the fish are trapped inside the net. Everyone is tense with excitement. A false step now could cost them the morning's work.

But Atorkor's fishermen are highly skilled, and the net, gleaming with silver scales, is hauled onto the sand.

The men throw out the unwanted jellyfish. Then they unload the net,

and the catch is arranged on the beach ready to be divided.

Children search among the discarded jellyfish for any small fish that may have been thrown out with them.

The empty net is spread out to dry and the men inspect it carefully for any signs of needed repairs.

Some take away so many fish they need help to lift the tubs onto their heads.

But the children who have helped the fishermen can easily carry their share in a small pan or on a string.

35

There is no refrigeration in Atorkor, and fresh fish spoils easily in the hot climate. So once the catch has been divided, the women hurry home to smoke or dry their fish.

When Kwabla gets out of
school at noon, his first chore is
to help his mother clean the fish.

Even his little sister lends a hand.

Kwabla's mother smokes most of the fish on a wire grate that fits over the oven.
She will also dry some of it and sell some fresh in the market.

By the time all the fish have been cleaned, Kwabla is very hungry and ready for lunch. Today Kwabla is making his favorite dish, fried cassava. Cassava is a root that is a very popular food in Ghana. Kwabla spices the cassava with red pepper, which he grinds on the stone mill.

Mealtime is informal in Atorkor. People eat whenever they like, and it is not unusual for boys to cook for themselves. Since families rarely eat together, the tables are very small. A few chickens are always close by, to pick up stray crumbs.

Occasionally there is more fishing in the afternoon, but usually the fishermen use this time to repair the net and coil the ropes in preparation for the next day's fishing.

Kwabla and his friend Akagbo are often on hand to help the men.

Most of the people of Atorkor, however, like to sit in the shade and talk during the hot hours of the afternoon. Sometimes they cut or braid each other's hair, or weave baskets to sell in the market.

45

On Monday morning, Kwabla's mother gets up early to make kenkey to sell in Keta, the main market town of the area. She also sells corn, onions, tomatoes, coconuts, and cassava from her husband's fields, as well as the fish that she buys or that the boys in the family earn for helping the fishermen.

Every Monday people from Atorkor and other villages make their way to Keta.

They come to the market by taxi, bus, truck, and boat, or on foot,
bringing their goods in enamel tubs and baskets of all kinds.

49

The marketplace is piled high with an immense variety of wares, including fish, fruit, vegetables, firewood, and coconut shells to be used for fuel.

In a separate lane, women sell earthen jars.

By midday the open marketplace is hot and everybody is very thirsty. Business is never slow for the people who sell soft drinks in Keta.

For the rest of the week, the village store in Atorkor supplies most of the needs of the people. When Kwabla's parents need things like sugar, soap, canned milk, needles, cigarettes, or matches, he only has to run a few hundred yards to get them.

One of Kwabla's jobs is to draw water from the well and wash dishes with his brother Kwasi.

Later Kwabla and Kofi pick tomatoes from the kitchen garden for dinner.

Kwabla knows how to weave a fence from palm leaves to enclose the family's fields, which lie outside the village.

60

Once a week Kwabla washes his clothes in the lagoon behind Atorkor. On this Saturday afternoon, his friend Akagbo came along, and they met another boy named Dzidzo, who paddled across the lagoon to fill his family's jars at the village well.

Fish are plentiful in the lagoon, and a fisherman can make a good catch there by using traps. When the fish come to feed on the leafy branches placed in front of the traps, the fisherman stretches a net around the branches, and the fish are caught inside.

63

Kwabla often goes to Keta on Saturday or Sunday to watch priests and priestesses perform tribal dances. The dancers are people who know the special, secret rites of the Ewe tribe. They are accompanied by musicians playing drums and other instruments.

65

68

Whenever Kwabla and his friends can, they head straight for the beach.

There they run races . . .

roll in the warm sand . . .
and splash in the roaring surf.

Often they play soccer or other ball games.

Whenever a fishing boat comes in sight offshore, they stop to watch it, and the game they like best of all is playing fishermen.

78

The boys are clever at making their own toys. They love things with wheels, and build remarkable trucks from milk cans and twigs held together by soft, round fruit.

They race their trucks on the road that runs through the village.

In Atorkor people build their houses slowly, adding to them when they have money and time.

For Kwabla and his friends, these unfinished houses make perfect playgrounds.

After a day of running, jumping, climbing, and swimming, the boys are always hungry. Kwabla sharpens a machete on the edge of his family's well, and climbs to the top of a palm tree to get a coconut.

One of his friends skillfully cuts into the sweet fruit.

85

In the evening, when the fires are burning low, Kwabla returns to the house he shares with Kofi. The boys are soon fast asleep, dreaming of the day when they will paddle the fishing boats into the ocean and strain at the ropes of the nets with the men of Atorkor.